Pearls

For the Personal Spiritual Journey

PEARLS OF LIFE
For the personal spiritual journey

Pearls of Life UK edition, English translation © 2006 Augsburg Fortress, Minneapolis, MN, USA

First published in hardcover edition 2007, reprinted 2008
Paperback edition first published 2013

Wild Goose Publications
4th Floor, Savoy House, 140 Sauchiehall Street, Glasgow G2 3DH, UK
www.ionabooks.com

Wild Goose Publications is the publishing division of the Iona Community. Scottish Charity No. SC003794. Limited Company Reg. No. SC096243.

ISBN 978-1-84952-283-0

© 2005 Verbum Förlag AB. Original edition published in Swedish under the title *Livets pärlor* by Verbum Förlag AB, Stockholm, Sweden.

A catalogue record for this book is available from the British Library.

Printed by Charlesworth Press, Wakefield, UK

BACKGROUND OF THIS BOOK

In the fall of 2004, Carolina Welin contacted Verbum Publishers with an idea for producing an inspirational book based on the popular prayer aid *Our Savior's Wreath.* The publishers were interested and this book, *Pearls of Life,* is the result.

Carolina Welin and Carolina Johansson wrote the text for the book. The pearl bracelet as well as the prayers and inspirational explanations for each pearl were written a decade earlier by Martin Lönnebo.

The pearls are handmade in India and purchased through a fair trade company called Tar Projects.

Martin Lönnebo is Bishop Emeritus of the Linkoping diocese of the Swedish Lutheran Church. Carolina Welin works in communications and marketing in Stockholm, Sweden. Carolina Johansson is a journalist and writer who also works in Stockholm.

Sometimes the entire expanse can be overwhelming.
We cannot comprehend the immensity.

Contents

What Are
the Pearls of Life?

I was impressed with the concept behind Bishop Martin Lönnebo's *Pearls of Life* the first time I saw it. Each little pearl, ascribed with its own unique personality, carries a deeper meaning for our lives.

Each pearl shares a message and bears an invitation from the creator—from God. The *Pearls of Life* make it possible for me to begin an inner conversation with God about my longings, my dreams, and my prayers. I always carry my *Pearls of Life* with me to remind me of what is most important in my life.

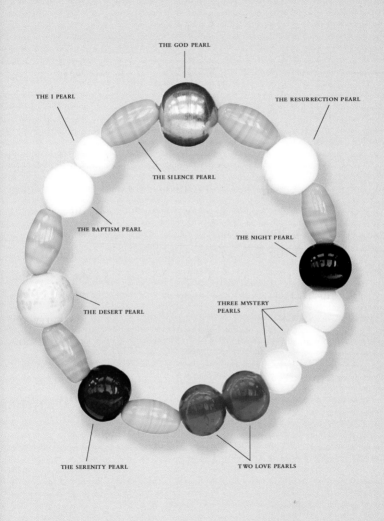

THE GOD PEARL

THE I PEARL

THE RESURRECTION PEARL

THE SILENCE PEARL

THE BAPTISM PEARL

THE NIGHT PEARL

THE DESERT PEARL

THREE MYSTERY
PEARLS

THE SERENITY PEARL

TWO LOVE PEARLS

LET THE *Pearls of Life*
BE YOUR COMPANION

The idea behind the *Pearls of Life* is simple. They are prayer pearls that remind us of what is most important in life: That I am a person who needs to breathe anew to live in peace and harmony with others, with nature, and with God.

Eighteen pearls. Twelve round, six oblong.

Hold them. Let the pearls slowly wind through your fingers, one after another. Think about what is important in your life.

What blesses me and brings me joy?

Where is my focus in life?

Is my focus where it should be?

Reflect upon this.

Our journey with the prayer pearls is symbolic of our journey through life. It isn't necessarily an easy journey. In the beginning we may resist. We don't hear the message the pearls bring us. We don't feel the connection. Be calm. The pearls help us focus on the present and not be concerned with what lies ahead. Each pearl has a meaning of its own. The purpose of the journey is to discover God, to reconnect with our inner self, and to better understand how we are connected to all humankind.

You can take the Pearls of Life with you everywhere you go. They will be your companions, and provide support when you need it.

WHY DO WE NEED
A SPIRITUAL COMPANION?

Our inner voice grows weak and our spirit becomes constricted. We live disjointed lives, continually distracted by interruptions throughout the course of the day. Our constant mobility can also cause stress. Researchers have begun to realize that these things are detrimental to our health and our sense of well-being.

We forget to block out the expectations and demands of the world around us. We forget our own needs. Sometimes it feels like we only exist for other people, and we feel guilty if we do something for ourselves. The world around us wants to be the center of our lives. Meaningful conversation is overpowered by television news, and work encroaches on family time. Even those who aren't employed are unable to enjoy their freedom, because the perceived notion that we must always be busy causes uncertainty. We become restless and discontented with our own lives, feeling we are existing, but not living. Even our feelings lack life. Our enthusiasm wanes, and our energy for life fizzles.

We need help. Sometimes we find support in our friends and family, people who see our needs and are there for us. But just as often we find ourselves alone and overwhelmed. We just can't make it. Suddenly it's all too much. We don't have time to deal with our own needs. We don't know which direction to go or how to get out of the constant rat race. This is when we need to look inward.

How do you find balance in your own life? That's easier said than done when you don't have adequate time. On the positive side, it doesn't require a lot of time—just a few minutes each day can go a long way. It's important to show yourself respect and love—to calm your mind and become introspective.

The *Pearls of Life* are spiritual companions that help you see beyond our shallow vision of what truly matters in life. Give them your questions, needs, and anxieties. Let the Desert Pearl be your companion when all is gloomy and dismal. Let the Love Pearls remind you of someone who blesses you. Create a place of joy and peace for a little while each day with the help of the God Pearl.

Pearls of Life —
COMPANIONS FOR EVERY DAY

The *Pearls of Life* help you express the deepest part of your humanity. At the same time, they are a bridge to God.

The *Pearls of Life* remind you to focus inwardly and encourage you to keep everything connected and to take one thing at a time. There is one pearl for every situation in your life.

The *Pearls of Life* give you time and show you a better way to live and to create balance between your need to have and your need to let go.

The *Pearls of Life* help you sort out your feelings, and in doing so help you grow in your awareness of what it truly means to live.

The pearls are introduced and explained on the following pages, but only you can decide which pearl means the most to you.

Carolina Welin

The Pearls

The God Pearl

THE GOD PEARL PRAYER

You are boundless;
You are near.
You are light
and I am yours.

The God Pearl

The golden pearl reminds us that there is someone who is always with us and watches over us. As the first and the last of the prayer pearls, the God Pearl represents the one who creates life and gives life meaning.

In the God Pearl you find the strength of one who holds all in his hand and the power of one who blesses you with all good things. The golden pearl symbolizes belief, wonder, and trust. Nothing is hopeless or meaningless when you find God.

What do I value in my life?

Do my days look as I want them to look?

Do I need to change anything?

The golden pearl reminds us of the value of our existence. This pearl is the invisible hand of God that holds us throughout our lives—God's holy presence.

We long for and dream of having a little time to ourselves every day. But we will never find quiet time for meditation if we don't intentionally carve out that moment in each day.

The God Pearl is the most beautiful, the largest, and the first of the prayer pearls. Caring. Loving. Unfathomable. It is just like God.

I can rest in God's peace with the God Pearl in my hand and I can feel that God is bearing my burdens. Any time during the day—while riding on a bus or in between appointments—I can put my hand in my pocket, touch the God Pearl, and be reassured that God welcomes and accepts me as I am. When my words are not enough, the God Pearl speaks for me.

MY THOUGHTS

The Silence Pearls

THE SILENCE PEARL PRAYER

In God's silence may I be—
quiet, still, craving nothing.

The Silence Pearls

Our lives are filled with busyness and stress. The Silence Pearls remind us of the importance of silence—of the importance of just being. In stillness, we connect with our inner self and allow it to speak to us. As we draw near to the eternal, words are unnecessary—but we have to stop in order to hear silence. Hold one of the Silence Pearls and breathe deeply. Let your thoughts drift away. Be grounded in peace. Take as long as you need.

The ultimate silence is not only heard, but felt. It can come to us while we are walking, or when we are sitting on the sofa relaxing. Suddenly we become aware of the silence all around us. Oh, it feels so nice to be quiet sometimes!

Finding your own calm and quiet place within yourself takes practice. You can train yourself "not"—not to feel, not to think, not to talk, not to worry. You can practice "being"—being restful; being away from noise, wants, words, and frenzy. Now and then during the day, take hold of a Silence Pearl and stop what you're doing. Feel yourself filled with peace as you forget about time and the day's activities. Feel silence permeate your whole being and welcome this moment of quiet communion with God.

MY THOUGHTS

The I Pearl

THE I PEARL PRAYER

I am a drop
in God's sea
that reflects the sky.

The I Pearl

The I Pearl addresses who we are when all pretenses are stripped away. The I Pearl, placed beside the God Pearl, reminds us that we are created in God's image—that we are in conversation with God and all Creation.

Just as a grain of sand has the potential to become a pearl, each of us has abilities just waiting to be awakened and expressed. Some people recognize this more than others. Sometimes we get hung up in negativity and focus only on our inadequacies and the things we cannot do.

The I Pearl wants to help us see beyond our limitations. It allows us to see ourselves through God's loving eyes as the cherished and priceless people we not only are, but must be allowed to be. When you are holding the I Pearl, embrace the rawest form of your self and acknowledge your own beauty.

God is in each and every one of us, but the relationship between God and me is different than God's relationship with you or with anyone else. Our I Pearl helps us remember our own sense of self—our own needs for love, joy, and purpose—when we struggle with trying times and resentment.

We must allow ourselves to take the good with the bad. Sometimes life takes a turn for the better and everything goes the way it's supposed to—someone I'm thinking about calls as I'm about to phone them, and I'm in touch with my senses and connected with life.

But then the illusion crumbles and life returns to normal. It's dull and sluggish and nothing goes the way I want. Every day presents a new problem, and the week ahead seems to go on forever. That's when I grasp the I Pearl that mirrors itself in the God Pearl. When I breathe deeply, listen inwardly, and pray the I Pearl prayer, I can feel the calming warmth slowly spreading throughout my body. My strength is restored, and I see my purpose with renewed energy. Thank God that I exist!

MY THOUGHTS

The Baptism Pearl

THE BAPTISM PEARL PRAYER

I am your child, my God,
help me grow,
help me mature.

The Baptism Pearl

The white pearl invites us to begin again. It contains the promise of unlimited grace and forgiveness. It assures us that it is never too late.

We all seek, more or less consciously, for assurance that our lives matter. In our longing for affirmation, we do things because we have to or to please others. The great white pearl tells us that we are good just as we are—we don't have to disguise ourselves. Baptism symbolizes our meeting with God, but also the beginning of faith and rebirth—to be like a child again, to begin life anew as seen through the wondering eyes of a child. Leave behind your feelings of guilt and obligation. Seek to live in trust and to see the good in life. Hold the Baptism Pearl and pray for the child within you.

Life goes on as it usually does without our having to think about it. We are busy getting to the next meeting on time or to the dinner that waits. Sometimes it feels like we exist more for others than for ourselves. It seems like the people around us don't have time for us—or that they don't recognize us for who we really are. This makes us sad and leaves us feeling empty. "Is this how life is supposed to be?" we wonder. We sense that we are losing ourselves and those we love. Then the Baptism Pearl comes to our aid and reminds us of the needs of our inner child.

Set aside adulthood, make room for the inner self, the playful and longing child. The Baptism Pearl makes it easier for you to go on—to be inspired and in contact with all of your possibilities.

MY THOUGHTS

The Desert Pearl

THE DESERT PEARL PRAYER

Cleanse me
so I will be clean.
Heal me
so I will be whole.

The Desert Pearl

The sand colored pearl symbolizes difficult times in our lives—times when life is like remote wasteland. We lack strength, we lack direction, we have no one to talk to. We feel the weight of the world pressing down on us—all is barren and fruitless.

Desert times cannot be avoided. They come sooner or later in everyone's life. The desert is a place of deprivation that forces us to focus on what is essential: *What must I have to live?*

It's hard to walk through the deserts of our own lives, but we can train ourselves to meet and survive our desert times. They can teach us to distinguish between the important and unimportant stuff of life. In retrospect we discover that our time in the desert has sharpened our perspective. When you hold the Desert Pearl, try to remember how you survived earlier desert times. Think, "What is it that allowed me to keep going?"

Life is filled with deserts—sand as far as the eye can see—places without hope. The beauty of the Desert Pearl is that it addresses these very real places in our lives. The desert can be an aimless wandering through everyday life, or a huge task that can only be traversed through hard work. It can be the apprehension and difficult recovery connected with being seriously ill. It can be a time of isolation.

There is only one way to face life's deserts, and that is head-on. There are no shortcuts or fast ways out. The Desert Pearl teaches you to practice patience. One more step, one more breath, one more blink of the eye, and little by little you begin to see tiny indications of life in the desert. If you accept that this is just the way it is right now, eventually you will see that progress is being made. The Desert Pearl reminds us that even in times of doubt and struggle God is with us, knows our need, and carries us when we can go no further. It is a steadfast coach encouraging, "Don't give up. Take one more step."

MY THOUGHTS

The Serenity Pearl

THE SERENITY PEARL
PRAYER

Help me really live,
not just exist.

The Serenity Pearl

The heavenly blue pearl is a rest stop. Here in peace and quiet, we are allowed to "be" without any need to "do."

On the other side of the desert, the Serenity Pearl offers us a place to stretch out and unwind. "What shall I do now?" we wonder. The blue pearl encourages us to ask, "What baggage can I get rid of?" In this serene moment nothing is holding us down. We can fly freely like the birds. This is a God-ordained moment of peace and quiet. Rest well. Be renewed by nature or the company of someone you like. When you hold the blue pearl, try to transport yourself to an emotional state where you lust for life.

The good times in life are wonderful. Here with every breath, we can enjoy God's creation and all living things. The little things that seem so important are really quite small in the scheme of things. We are, after all, part of a greater whole.

What matters most in life isn't always measured in time, but in experiences, love, joy, and fellowship. This pearl addresses our yearnings for harmony, balance, and connection. We need to stop and take comfort in our Serenity Pearl more often. Although it can seem a distraction to pause for a Serenity Pearl moment during difficult times, this is exactly when we need it. Here we can practice living in the NOW. Live, enjoy, and be glad that life contains a little allowance of time when we are free from obligations. The theme of the Serenity Pearl is Carpe Diem. Seize the day. The time is now.

MY THOUGHTS

The Love Pearls

THE FIRST LOVE PEARL
PRAYER

Open me now
to the strength of love I long for.

There Are Two Love Pearls

All life encompasses love—and love, like our breath, moves in two ways—in and out. Therefore, there are two Love Pearls. To love and be loved is life's awesome gift.

The first pearl is about accepting love—being open to love when it comes to us. That in itself can be pretty hard. The second pearl is the love we share. Love is being there for others and giving of ourselves regardless of what we get in return. When you hold the red pearls, think about the love in your life—the love you receive and the love you give.

THE FIRST PEARL IS FOR THE LOVE WE RECEIVE

A loving gesture or gift from another person makes us happy, but perhaps it instills a sense of being in debt as well. We wonder, "Do I now owe this person something in return?"

We need to feel the emotional connection between one another more often. We are worth loving. To be embraced by another—to be enveloped in love—lends immeasurable strength. Breathe deeply, feel the nearness of nature, and allow yourself to be enfolded by the warmth and the light. Let go of the cares of everyday life and grip the first Love Pearl. Send a prayer of thanks for everything you have and for everything you are part of. In love.

MY THOUGHTS

THE SECOND LOVE PEARL
PRAYER

God, help me love.

THE SECOND PEARL IS FOR THE LOVE WE GIVE

Both pearls remind us of those we love. We think of loved ones who are near to us and of those far away whom we may not have seen for a long time. We think of those who help us everyday and of those who have gone before us. Love is a gift. The more you share it, the more it grows.

The unfathomable love of God, greater than any human love, brings us closer to God and to one another. The second Love Pearl reminds me of God's love alive in me. I hold it closer and I can see you. You are real to me.

MY THOUGHTS

The Mystery Pearls

THE MYSTERY PEARLS PRAYER

Large or small,
I entrust the secrets of my heart
to your care.

The Mystery Pearls

Three small white pearls hide the innermost secrets of the heart. These are the things that we don't share with anyone, or that we don't know how to express.

Some secrets are thoughts and desires that we carry inside. Some are experiences that we've either witnessed or been part of that are too difficult to talk about, but will be with us forever. People are a mystery, and sometimes we don't even understand ourselves. There is a place for our secrets in these pearls. Here our secrets are safe. The pearls have room for even the most precious people whom we think about and pray for—our loved ones who are sick, our children, our parents, and others who need attention. To hold the Mystery Pearls is to say:

God, remember them.

Don't forget them.

The question "Why?" can be troubling. We seek answers to life's mysteries, although we know deep down inside that there isn't always an answer for the things that happen.

There are things we don't understand—experiences we have no words for, secrets we want to bare and secrets we cannot share. Secrets are hard. Perhaps we fear that they will separate us from those we love. Our secrets might be promises that can't be broken, very private feelings, or our deepest concerns for our children and family members. God is always there for us to share our secrets—in light and in darkness. Perhaps we may see our deepest secrets as our most private meetings with God?

MY THOUGHTS

The Night Pearl

THE NIGHT PEARL PRAYER

Be close to me in darkness
so I find the light.

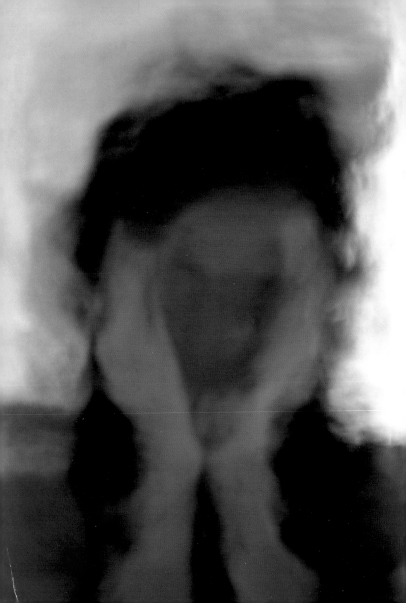

The Night Pearl

The black pearl is for life's darkest times—times of agony and doubt, fear and abandonment—times that drain our strength and courage. The Night Pearl holds our feelings of despair over senseless death and catastrophe—the things that make us wonder, "Is there a God?"

Don't hold back. Let your feelings out. It's necessary to pause for the darkness. There's light in the dark even if we don't always see it. It's always darkest before the light. When you hold the Night Pearl, give a moment to the darkness. Remember, even in the darkness God comes to you. You are never abandoned.

I cannot breathe. My mind is vacant. I'm locked in a nightmare of darkness. I break out in a cold sweat and tumble into the bottomless pit. No help can reach because I have never been so far away. I don't know where I am—I am completely lost. All is confusion. There are no paths that lead to help. I am falling. There is no hand to rescue me, no words to comfort me. The walls are closing in. There is no escape.

I am as alone as it is possible to be. Help me—anyone! The days have lost their structure. Time moves painfully slow. I do not recognize myself. Where is the person I used to be? What has become of my spirit? Is this really me— closed off and directionless? I can't bring myself to do anything. I'm hovering between being fed up and giving up. The struggle is getting worse. I'm alone. But through all this, I'm still breathing. In the inhaling and exhaling of breath, I understand what the Night Pearl is all about. I grasp it and find a little respite from my spiritual chaos. There is a God. God is with me. I am exhausted, but I am not alone.

MY THOUGHTS

The Resurrection Pearl

THE RESURRECTION PEARL
PRAYER

Every breath
you in me
me in you.

The Resurrection Pearl

The white pearl stands for good's defeat of evil, hope's victory over despair, and life's conquest of death.

The night is over. Morning has come. The shadows fade and disappear. There is nothing difficult now. That which we thought was unreachable is now near. The light isn't gone, after all. It's within me and shining out through me. This is the pearl of peace where we rest after the night.

The Resurrection Pearl gives us hope when life opposes us. In the midst of our worries over what is and what is to come, this pearl wants to remind us of the potential for good to conquer evil, and of the importance of seeking the light. Never give up hope. Hope is ignited when you hold onto this pearl and pray for renewal.

Suddenly—sunrise! The light returns. One after another the puzzle pieces fall into place until all at once I can see the whole picture. Finally. I'm back in touch. I can trust again. I open my eyes. The colors have returned. Smells. People. Love—your love—my love. All is complete. All is calm. I am here and you are with me.

MY THOUGHTS

Background on the Pearls of Life

The *Pearls of Life* came to be on a small island in the Greek Isles. It was late summer when Martin Lönnebo, recently retired from his work as bishop in the Linkoping diocese of the Swedish Lutheran Church, embarked on a Mediterranean cruise to read and enjoy himself. A sudden unseasonable storm forced the ship to dock in the harbor of a small island inhabited by just forty-seven people. Martin Lönnebo found a room in which to wait out the storm, and it was there that he began to develop the idea that would become *Our Savior's Wreath* or the *Pearls of Life.*

Perhaps he was inspired by the nearness of the sea, because Martin sometimes describes the pearls as a life buoy that can be used to keep us afloat when the currents of our lives change, drowning us in demands, expectations, and information. That's when we need something to hold on to that will help us focus and draw us back to what is most important in our lives.

Although the *Pearls of Life* came into being in just a few days, the idea behind them took shape gradually in Martin's mind. For a long time, he had been looking for a way to help busy people reconnect with their inner self and find answers to the spiritual longings they didn't know how to address.

Martin is convinced that every person is comprised of body, mind, and spirit. But contemporary society ignores the spiritual and focuses on the material. While we think we have what we need with food, home, and possessions, we find it increasingly difficult to find meaning in such things. Is this really where life's meaning is found? Martin believes that people want to live in life's center, but move constantly to the periphery. Then after a while, they are tempted to believe that the periphery is the center they seek. Our basic needs have been taken care of, giving us a certain sense of security, but this is not enough to keep us from wondering about God. Is there holiness? Eternity? Is there a loving cosmic force that holds all things together? The answers to these questions demand time . . . attention . . . and more time.

After thinking about it, Martin concluded that any means to help people deal with these questions would need to meet four criteria. It must include prayer. It must be tangible. It must guide us in our journey with Christ. And it must be easy to use and to understand.

People today are overwhelmed, living with regrets about the past and worries about the future. Life seems only an accumulation of the things we've accomplished or the things that we need to do. Consequently, we never really live in the present. What shall we do? Martin says we sit down, light a candle, perhaps, and reflect on what is important in life. Do we need something to help us focus? We grasp the pearls and allow them to slowly wind between our fingers. And so we begin. Pastor Lönnebo freely admits that the pearls were developed partly out of his own need for focus in his spiritual life. There are things we can do, like taking a deep breath and focusing on our breathing, that help us reach a state of tranquility. Meditation helps us pray.

Martin writes in his book *Our Savior's Wreath* that for a variety of reasons he himself had not found time for regular prayer and meditation. "It can be difficult to pray," he says. This is a surprising confession from someone who has lived his entire life in a spiritual calling.

Martin Lönnebo was born in Vasterbottniska Kagetrask in 1930. As the eighth and last child of a farmer, he grew up with animals and nature. It was outside beside the sea that seven-year-old Martin first became aware that everything around him was only part of something much greater. He sensed that he was in God's presence and this is where he belonged.

For a short time in his youth, Martin worked as a farm hand and also as a charcoal maker. When offered the opportunity to attend the university, Martin initially studied philosophy, but soon switched to theology—eventually earning a doctor's degree. He was ordained a pastor before turning thirty, and served several congregations before being appointed Bishop of the Linkoping Diocese, where he served until his retirement in 1995. In spite of his religious background, Martin is the first to admit that prayer and faith are not simple. "Just look at me," he says. "If you think as I do that it is difficult to become focused in prayer, then one needs to find a means to help us focus."

Martin Lönnebo lives simply with his wife, Britt Louise, in a townhouse in the suburbs of Linkoping. Several large icons hang along the path near his home. Creation unfolds in the garden outside his front window. Seven reflecting orbs, one for each day of the week, create a place to practice meditation and contemplate creation. Martin always carries his pearls with him and whenever he touches them, he is reminded of

God's presence. This tactile reminder grounds him and helps him remember the ultimate value of life.

His relationship with God is central for Martin. A co-worker has described him as a man who is in the world but not of the world. While Martin says that the *Pearls of Life* will help us find God, he acknowledges that they will also help us reconnect with our inner self, our fellow human beings, and with nature. This spiritual journey isn't easy. It requires faith, which is beyond understanding, and that can be very frightening. Our walk with God isn't a single experience, but a journey, and Martin speaks often about the importance of spiritual training for the journey. Just as our bodies need exercise and our minds need intellectual stimulus, so we must take time to nurture our spiritual selves. Spiritual training may sound like work, but it is very important. We develop and maintain our relationship with God through regular prayer and meditation. We will come to know God through prayer, not through reason. It all begins with God, ourselves, and a time for silence.

Our journey with the *Pearls of Life* began with the God Pearl, then the I Pearl, and next the Silence Pearl. After these came the pearls for birth (the Baptism Pearl), death (the Night Pearl, and rebirth (the Resurrection Pearl). The prayer pearls are eighteen pearls counting the six Silence Pearls. Many people wonder about the configuration—why there are three Mystery Pearls, or six Silence Pearls, or twelve round pearls. Martin says, "The eighteen pearls have less meaning than the twelve round pearls which symbolize the gates to heaven mentioned in Revelation 21:21. (And the twelve gates are twelve pearls, each of the gates is a single pearl, and the street of the city is pure gold, transparent as glass.) Every pearl is a gate waiting to be opened. "But I can always tell you that six is the number for the human being—the restless being that needs peace—and eighteen (10 + 8) is the number of completion."

Perhaps the three Mystery Pearls also need a little explanation. Originally, Martin thought of giving one pearl to each of his three children, but that's not what happened. Instead, he ascribed his children and all the rest of his loved ones, living and dead, to the first Mystery Pearl. He thinks of it as a large, white, beautiful house for them to live in. "But I am glad there finally were three Mystery Pearls," he says. "Three, you see, is the number of community and of God."

If there is one pearl that Martin hesitated to include, it is the Night pearl. It wasn't part of the first circle of pearls because he feared what it represented—darkness, agony, crisis, doubt, and death—would be too much to bear. But although he hesitated initially, Martin now believes that the black pearl is essential. Death cannot be avoided. It is a part of life. Only by losing this life can we inherit a better life.

Martin tells a story about when he and two friends were lost on a desert island, and the terror that came over them. Fearing that they were about to die, they didn't worry about the things they hadn't accomplished, but thought instead about how they hadn't kept in touch with those they loved and who loved them. Martin began to think about his family, and suddenly he knew that he had to find a way to survive. His first thoughts were about his son Jonas. He sensed that Jonas still needed time with his father and he knew he had to give him that time. "Perhaps," Martin said later, "the will to live is inspired by our fear of death, by our belief that we have something left to accomplish, or by our desire to live a better life. The finality of death helps us value life. Recognizing your own mortality forces you to see a reality larger than the present. Therefore I included the Night pearl because, like death, it is part of life."

After returning from Greece, Martin strung his first circle of wooden beads and tried it out. It worked, but it wasn't well accepted. Some people thought it was childish. Others thought there was something suspicious—something mystical—about it. It reminded them of a magic charm. Martin notes that prayer in its deepest form is magic in that it

Bishop Martin Lönnebo

seeks transformation, but the skeptics weren't convinced. Martin acknowledges that the pearls are simplistic, but points out that the simplest things often bring joy. What matters is that it works. What is its secret? Its simplicity appeals to people, as does its beauty. But Martin emphasizes that it is its tangible nature that gives him strength. As Martin explains, we can write books about God, listen to people talk about God, but being present with God is beyond words, and is all about wanting to touch and be touched. It has been ten years since the first Pearls of Life were created, and today they are used diligently and often. They have helped countless people find deeper meaning in prayer and in their relationship with God. When Martin is asked if the popularity of the *Pearls of Life* surprises him, he responds, "No, it makes me happy."

The reason for the popularity is that both the book and the pearls themselves carry the same simple message. Martin says that the Pearls of Life have given him something money can't buy. They have enriched his prayer life and his relationship to God. Perhaps the book could have made Martin wealthy, but early on he and his wife decided that they would give the royalties from both the book and the pearls to Individuell Manniskohjalp (IM), through whom the Lönnebos have established a fund for handicapped children in honor of their son Jonas. For them, living with a child with autism has been a challenge and a sorrow, but at the same time a gift and a source of learning and inspiration. "Just as you can love life without understanding it, our relationship with God doesn't exist on an intellectual plane. It lives way outside of that—in a beauty and comfort beyond understanding," says Martin Lönnebo.

Carolina Johansson